PLEASE

PASS THE

DOODLES

DEBORAH ZEMKE

BLUE 🍎 APPLE

PLEASE PASS THE SQUIGGLES.

Here are some of the lines and shapes you'll use to draw rhinos, cowboys, anteaters and more!

Squiggle

Arch

ELLIPSE

An ellipse is a squashed circle. Look what happens to this cake. Looking at it from the top, you see a circle. As you squash the circle, it changes your whole point of view.

Wedge

Angle

Loop

Zigzag

Curves

Loopy fingers

Slice

Curve hook

DON'T BE A PICKY EATER

Talk about picky! Koalas only eat one thing—eucalyptus leaves. They don't even drink water, just eucalyptus juice. So you might think that eucalyptus leaves would be as good as ice cream. In fact, they're tough to chew and toxic to digest—unless you're a koala!

Finish designing the menu for the Koala Café.

DRAW A KOALA. Put this picky eater in the oval on your menu.

1) Draw a squiggly O.

1) Add two squiggly ears...

3) a squiggly G...

4) a curve, and two V's.

5) Make loopy hands and a loopy foot.

6) Draw a koala nose in the middle of a happy face.

7) Put your koala in its favorite all-you-can-eat treeside restaurant.

WRITE the Special for today. What will it be? A eucalyptus burger? Or a eucalyptus shake? Make up your own krazy koala dish and draw a picture of it in the box.

KOALA CAFÉ

SPECIAL TODAY

DRAW a border of eucalyptus leaves.

EAT EVERYTHING ON YOUR PLATE . . .
but don't eat the plate.

Talk about not picky! Goats nibble on just about anything, including paper plates. Goats are great eaters and nimble climbers.

1) Add two horns to the snout.

2) Draw a loopy ear and an elliptical eye.

3) Make a squiggly jaw...

4) and curvy back.

5) Use short curves to make a tail and beard.

6) Add lots of curves for fur...

7) and four wedges for feet.

DRAW TWO GOATS,
a bigger one on the mountain in front and a smaller one on the mountain in back.

Add some bushes for the goats to eat and some clouds in the sky.

Start drawing here.

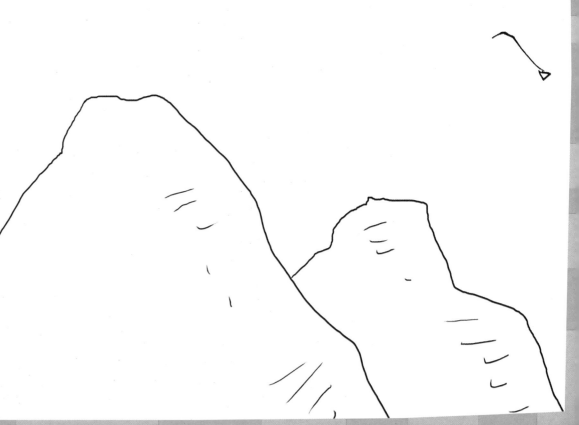

CHEW YOUR FOOD BEFORE YOU SWALLOW.

Unless you're a snake! Snakes don't have the teeth for chewing—or the claws for tearing—their food into bite-size pieces. But they do have amazing expandable jaws, so they can swallow food that's bigger than their heads.

DRAW your own snake pattern for Betty's twin, Buster, and give him something good to swallow.

HOW MANY burgers did Betty the Boa eat?

Betty ate a bike!

DRAW something else that Betty ate.

DRAW the pattern on Betty's back.

DON'T HAVE A COW!

Don't have a tantrum at the table just because you're having rutabaga ratatouille for the third day in a row.

DO HAVE A COW!

Drink your milk, which comes from thousands of Holstein dairy cows, each with its own black and white markings.

DRAW a different black and white design for each cow and write her name underneath.

Here are some ideas:

Bessie

Dotty

Daisy

Why did the cow go to Hollywood?

To be in the mooooovies.

What did she star in?

Romeo and Moooliet.

Cowtoon

WRITE your own cowtoon in the bubbles.

WASH YOUR PAWS
before you eat.

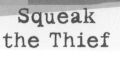

Someone got into the cookie jar and took the last cookie. Can you identify the thief from the pawprints left behind? Here's a clue: Cats and mice walk on their tiptoes. Raccoons walk on flat feet.

DRAW each suspect in its box. Then draw bars over the one that you think is the cookie thief.

Robber Raccoon

Squeak the Thief

Kitty Burglar

Robber Raccoon

1) Draw two arched ears and a squiggle.

2) Add two beady eyes in triangles.

3) Draw a black T nose and line.

4) Add three squiggly curves.

5) Make two arms and four paws with claws.

6) Add a striped tail and fur.

Squeak the Thief

1) Draw two loopy ears.

2) Add two staring eyes...

3) and a V-button nose.

4) Draw angle arms and...

5) loopy legs and toes.

6) Add a curvy tail and whiskers.

Kitty Burglar

1) Draw two pointy ears, a squiggle...

2) two watchful eyes...

3) a T-nose and five curves.

4) Draw four squiggly curves...

5) four lines and four paws.

6) Add a curvy tail, whiskers and stripes.

Don't **STUFF** your face!

Chipmunks stuff their cheeks with seeds and nuts, but they don't eat them all at once. Instead, they bury their goodies to eat later in the winter.

1) Draw a curvy curve.

2) Attach two curves.

3) Make an eye, nose and whiskers.

4) Add a squiggly C.

  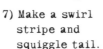

5) Draw a 2 and three V's.

6) Add loopy fingers and toes.

7) Make a swirl stripe and squiggle tail.

DRAW CHIP.

Chip has forgotten where he put his stash of six acorns. Use the clues to find where each acorn is located and put it in the picture. The first one is done for you.

1. Don't kick! One acorn is between the pine tree and the soccer ball.
2. See red! One is between the house and the tree with red leaves.
3. Mellow yellow! One is between the worm and the tree with yellow leaves.
4. Swing low! One is underneath the swing.
5. Meow, bow-wow! One is between the cat and the white dog.
6. Welcome home! One is under the welcome mat.

DRAW CHIP'S ACORNS.

DON'T TAKE FOOD

FROM SOMEONE ELSE'S PLATE.

What's missing? Each of these four plates should have the same four foods on it.

DRAW the missing food on each plate.

DRAW a design on the tablecloth.

DON'T EAT DESSERT FIRST!

Don't be a bee! Bees eat dessert first and last! In fact, the only thing they eat is sweet—the sweet nectar of flowers. If you were a bee, what kind of sweet flowers would you like? How about an ice cream coneflower?

DRAW A BEE

 1) Draw two ellipses and a C.

 2) Add two curves and a triangle.

 3) Attach a squiggly C...

 4) and six squiggly legs.

 5) Make three C curves....

6) and squiggly stripes.

DRAW your favorite sweets on the plants in this garden.

It's a B of bees!

HELP PUT DINNER ON THE TABLE

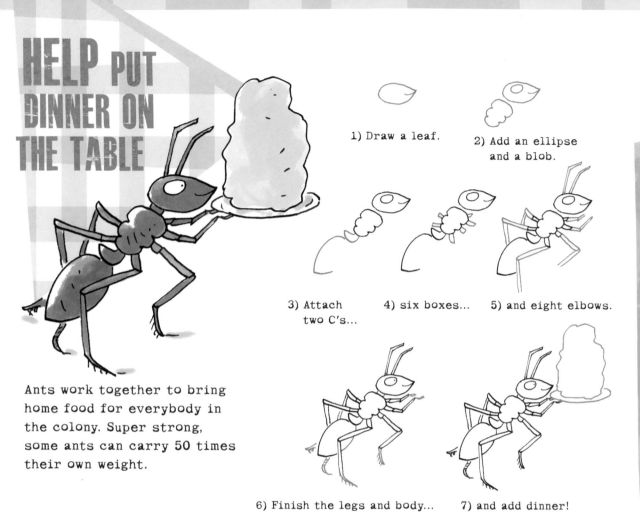

Ants work together to bring home food for everybody in the colony. Super strong, some ants can carry 50 times their own weight.

DRAW AN ANT.

1) Draw a leaf.

2) Add an ellipse and a blob.

3) Attach two C's...

4) six boxes...

5) and eight elbows.

6) Finish the legs and body...

7) and add dinner!

This ant is late with dinner. Help it find its way to the table.

An octopus doesn't need a knife or fork to dig into its favorite seafood. It breaks open clams, crabs, snails and scallops with its mouth, which is—unlike the rest of the squishy octopus—as hard as a bird's beak.

DRAW A SCALLOP.

1) Draw a curvy U. 2) Connect with a squiggle curve. 3) Add two small curves.

DRAW A CLAM.

1) Draw a small curve. 2) Add a C... 3) and a backwards C. 4) Draw a curve.

DRAW A SNAIL.

1) Draw a small C. 2) Add a backwards C. 3) Make two loops... 4) and a curve.

DRAW A CRAB.

1) Draw a shield 2) Add two pairs of curves. 3) Attach ten zigzags... 4) and ten more zigzags. 5) Draw two claws in front.

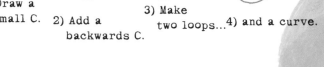

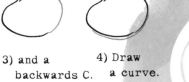

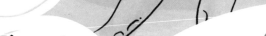

SCALLOP

USE A KNIFE AND A FORK.

CLAM

SNAIL

CRAB

DON'T PLAY WITH YOUR FOOD.

Hey, dude.
California sea lions
love to play.
They float, fish
and even surf.

DRAW A SEA LION.

1) Draw a
   curvy head.

2) Add a
   curvy chest...

3) eye, ear, nose
   and whiskers.

4) Draw two
   curvy, squiggly
   flippers...

5) a curve belly ...

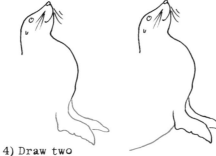

6) curvy back and leg...

7) and loopy flippers.

What is your sea lion
balancing on its nose?

DON'T REACH ACROSS THE TABLE FOR SECONDS.

It's a frog's life—first, an egg, then a tadpole, and finally, a high jumping, fly-catching grown-up frog! Finish Froggy's photo album.

Why did Froggy play center field?

To catch flies.

DRAW FROGGY THE CENTER FIELDER.

Make up your own picture of Froggy catching a baseball.

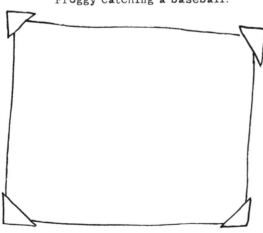

DRAW FROGGY THE TADPOLE.

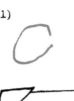 1) 2) 3)   4)

Froggy!

Froggy is one egg in a million!

He hatched!

Froggy's first legs!

He comes up for air.

His first hop ashore!

DRAW FROGGY ON A LILY PAD.

Froggy's first fly!

 1) Draw two dotted O's.

 2) Add a zig...

3) and three curves.

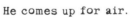 4) Make loopy fingers...

 5) loopy feet...

 6) and a long loopy tongue.

DON'T PUT YOUR ELBOWS ON THE TABLE...

Especially if you're a white rhino, which can weigh up to 7,000 pounds, as much as a pickup truck.

DRAW A RHINO.

DRAW A TRUCK.

 1) Draw seven toenails.

 2) Attach six squiggly lines...

3) and six curves.

 4) Add a curvy V head...

5) and two horns.

 6) Draw ears, eye and nostril.

 7) Add a curvy back...

 8) and tail.

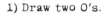 1) Draw two O's.

2) Put an angled line above.

3) Attach two angled lines at either end.

 4) Add a V and a loop.

 5) Draw an angled loop.

6) Add doors, bumpers, handle, lights and mirror.

Don't HOG the cake.

DRAW A CAKE.

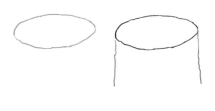

1) Draw a squiggly ellipse.

2) Attach two squiggly lines...

3) and two curves.

4) Add candles and your favorite icing...and draw a hog making a wish ...and balloons... and presents.

DRAW YOUR PIECE OF CAKE.

1) Draw a squiggly triangle. The bigger the triangle, the bigger your piece of cake.

2) Add a squiggly 7...

3) a squiggly loop and squiggly L.

4) Put it on a plate...

5) and eat it with a fork.

DON'T SLURP!

Dogs drink by lapping water with their tongues up into their mouths—and down all over the floor.

DRAW MY DOG.

1) Draw two eyes.

2) Make a T nose and snout.

3) Add squiggly ears...

4) and squiggle down to a curved back.

5) Make two furry front legs...

6) a furry tummy, two back legs...

7) and a furry tail.

DRAW A COOL DOG.

1) Draw a T nose...

2) with a smile.

3) Add sunglasses...

4) loopy ears...

5) and a collar.

6) Put your cool dog in a cool car.

DRAW A HOT DOG.

1) Draw a squiggle of mustard...

2) and a squiggle of ketchup.

3) Add two hot dog ends...

4) and put it in a bun.

DON'T
BURP!

And you know why! It stinks.

But sheep burps are worse than smelly because sheep belch methane gas. In a place like Australia, where there are some 80 million sheep, too much burping could harm the environment.

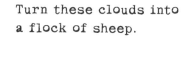

Turn these clouds into a flock of sheep.

DRAW three side views.

DRAW three front views.

DRAW one back view.

Give each of your sheep a name and write it underneath.

Here's the start of a sheepy alphabet. Turn the first letter of your name into a sheep.

Do not hiss, hoot, howl, growl, or roar—
NO MATTER HOW HUNGRY YOU ARE.

DRAW A HOOT.

Hoot owls are also known as barred owls. They hunt at night but hoot day and night. Some people think that their calls sound like, *Who cooks for you? Who cooks for you?*

1) Draw two curls...

2) and two bigger curls.

3) Add two dots, a V...

4) a half circle...

5) and two curves.

6) Make four lines...

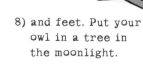

7) feathers...

8) and feet. Put your owl in a tree in the moonlight.

DON'T MAKE FUNNY FACES.

Don't make your food
into funny faces.

Chimps make lots of funny faces,
and sad ones, too.
Sometimes when it looks
like a chimp is smiling,
it's really scared out
of its wits. Chimps
also call, hug, kiss,
and shake hands.

MAKE A FUNNY FACE
MADE OUT OF FOOD.

DRAW YOUR FACE.

ENGAGE IN PLEASANT CONVERSATION.

Would you go near the mouth of a crocodile?
A bird called the Egyptian plover steps right inside a
crocodile's mouth. Why? To eat! It snacks on
tasty tidbits in the croc's mouth
and the croc opens wide---
and stays open wide---
to get its teeth cleaned.

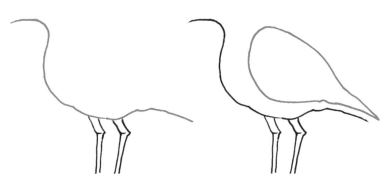

1) Attach a curve to the bird legs.

2) Add a teardrop wing...

3) a curvy S...

4) and four curves.

Here's what the plover's feet look like.

Don't squawk with your mouth **FULL**.

Polly may want a cracker, but a parrot usually eats nuts, seeds and fruit, so its mouth is designed for more than talking. Its beak is a nutcracker, crow bar, wedge, spike, vise, and pincers, all in one super eating tool.

Do you want to squawk like a parrot when your mouth is NOT full? Try saying this very fast, five times:

Polly Parrot pared a pair of pretty pears.

WRITE your own tongue twister:

DRAW A BEAK.

DRAW A NUTCRACKER.

DRAW PINCERS.

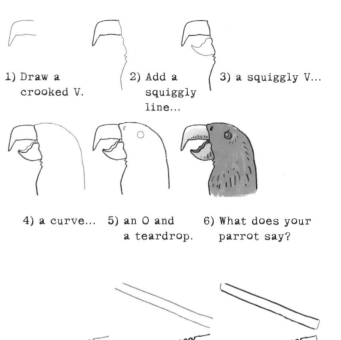

1) Draw a crooked V. 2) Add a squiggly line... 3) a squiggly V...

4) a curve... 5) an O and a teardrop. 6) What does your parrot say?

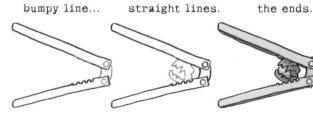

1) Draw one bumpy line... 2) and three straight lines. 3) Connect the ends.

4) Add two curves, two O's... 5) and a nut.

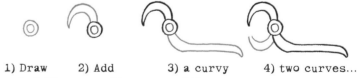

1) Draw two O's. 2) Add a slice... 3) a curvy loop... 4) two curves...

5) a curvy loop... 6) and a berry.

SIT UP STRAIGHT IN YOUR CHAIR.

What has four legs but can't run? Your chair not only has four legs, it's got a seat for your seat and a back for your back.

Who says I can't run?

DRAW A CHAIR.

DRAW A FANCY CHAIR.

Draw your chair. Draw the chair you're sitting on—or make up your own chair design.

1) Draw the seat.
2) Draw the legs.
3) Draw the back.

1) Draw a squashed diamond.

2) Attach a V with three lines...

3) four loops down...

1) Draw an ellipse.

2) Attach three curves...

3) four curvy loops..

4) two longer loops up...

5) and connect with four lines.

4) one big loop, two curvy curves...

5) one super curvy curve...

6) and another one flip-flopped.

SIT DOWN
IN YOUR CHAIR!

Who jumps higher, man or beast?
Both could dunk a basketball into
a hoop ten feet off the ground—if
a kangaroo could hold a basketball.

DRAW A KANGAROO. Add to the face.

1) Add three
curves...

2) four
V's...

3) two
more V's...

4) five more
curves...

5) loopy fingers
and toes and
a big tail.

DRAW A SLAM DUNK. Add to the arm.

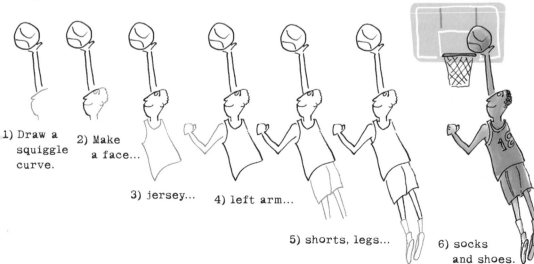

1) Draw a
squiggle
curve.

2) Make
a face...

3) jersey...

4) left arm...

5) shorts, legs...

6) socks
and shoes.

WIPE YOUR MOUTH
WITH A NAPKIN.

You're having guests for dinner.

DESIGN a napkin for each one.

Niles Crocodile

Stretch the Giraffe

Elliephant

Stripey Zebra

Squeak the Mouse

Froggy

Don't throw food.

Don't throw any food, but especially don't throw a live fish, even if you catch it in your beak like a heron.

DRAW A HERON.

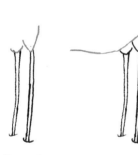

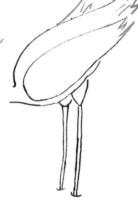

1) Draw two U's on the skinny legs sticking out of the pond.

2) Draw a curve...

3) a C and another curve.

4) Add ziggy feathers...

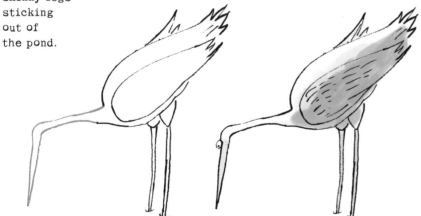

5) two elbow curves...

6) an eye and go fish!

Which two fish are the same kind? Add some more fish to the pond.

BE POLITE

Remember to say "please" and "thoink you".

Thoinks!

If you're at home, take off your shoe and sock.

This little piggy went to market.

This little piggy stayed home.

This little piggy ate roast beef.

This little piggy had none.

This little piggy cried all the way home.

DRAW your own five little piggies in the space below. If you're not at home, draw this foot.

DRAW your favorite foods in the basket.

DRAW what this little piggy is doing at home.

DRAW the monster making this little piggy cry.

DRAW the piggy holding the beef.

WRITE what the piggy with none says in the bubble.

CHEW YOUR FOOD, NOT THE TABLE.

Smile! A beaver and a cat have very different teeth, because they eat different kinds of food. A beaver's four front teeth are big and orange and made to cut wood. A cat has four very sharp front teeth called canines, which it uses to stab and grab. Who eats plants, and who eats meat?

DRAW AN HERBIVORE,
an animal that only eats plants.

DRAW A CARNIVORE,
an animal that only eats meat.

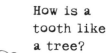

How is a tooth like a tree? They both have roots!

1) Draw the nose...

2) eyes,

3) ears...

4) cheeks, chin...

5) fur and hair.

HERBIVORE   CARNIVORE

DON'T LICK YOUR PLATE.

An aardvark has a long, sticky tongue so that it can reach into termite mounds and catch dinner.

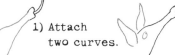

1) Attach two curves.

2) Add two ears, an eye...

3) squiggly arms...

4) a squiggly back...

5) two squiggly legs...

6) claws and a curvy tail.

DRAW AN AARDVARK

and then help this hungry critter catch the last termite in the mound. Start here:

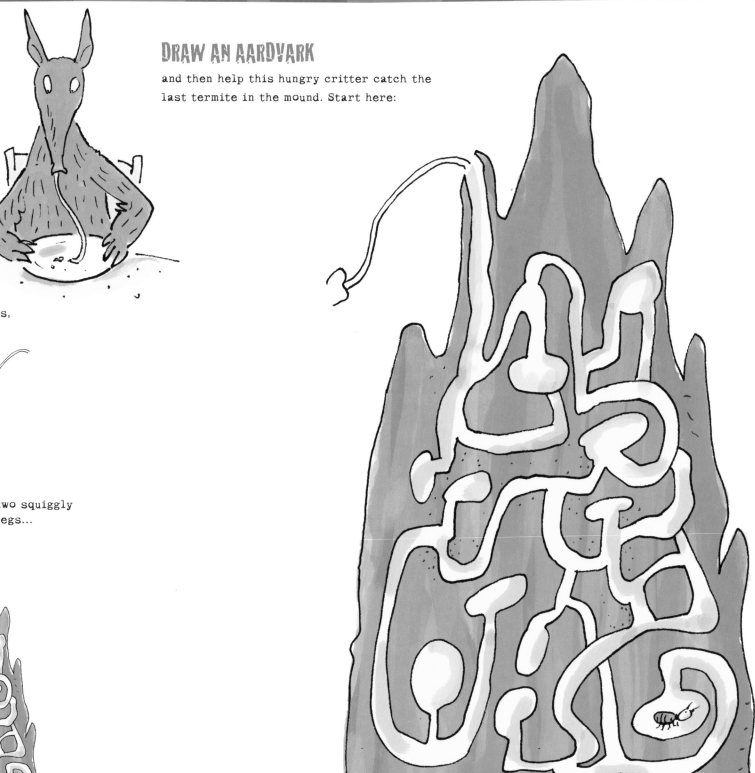

COME TO DINNER ON TIME.

1) Add an eye and snout to the helmet and goggles.

2) Draw a scarf.

3) Attach a bumpy curve...

4) two wavy lines...

5) seven straight lines...

6) and eight wedges.

7) Draw six curves...

8) claws and a tail.

DRAW A TORTOISE.

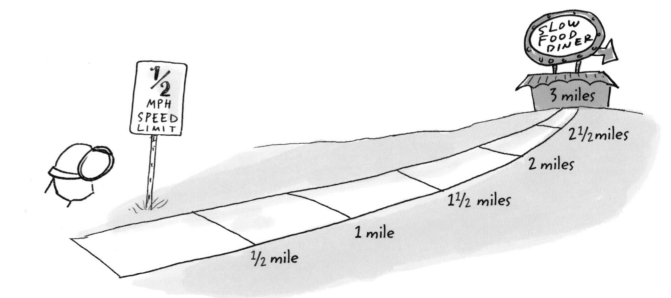

SLOW FOOD DINER

½ MPH SPEED LIMIT

3 miles

2½ miles

2 miles

1½ miles

1 mile

½ mile

DON'T FIGHT OVER THE LAST STRAND OF SPAGHETTI.

There are places at the feeder for Mr. Goldfinch and Mr. Cardinal, and enough seed to feed them, too!

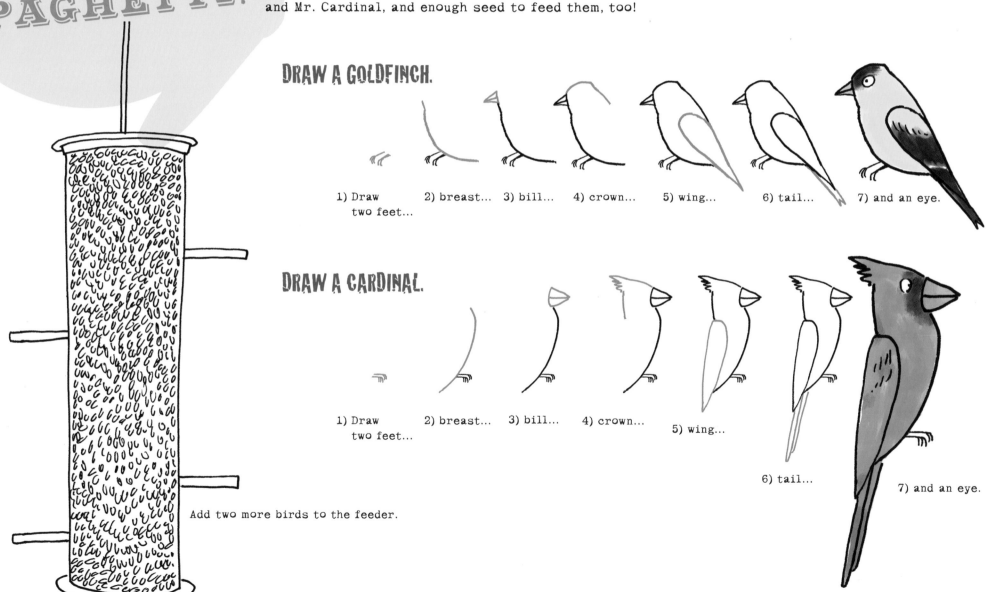

DRAW A GOLDFINCH.

1) Draw two feet...   2) breast...   3) bill...   4) crown...   5) wing...   6) tail...   7) and an eye.

DRAW A CARDINAL.

1) Draw two feet...   2) breast...   3) bill...   4) crown...   5) wing...   6) tail...   7) and an eye.

Add two more birds to the feeder.

CUT YOUR FOOD INTO BITE-SIZE PIECES.

DRAW LEO.

Leo's picture was cut into six squares, then four of the squares got mixed up. Put the pieces back together by drawing what's in each square in the correct blue square. After you've drawn Leo, decorate the frame.

I'm not lyin', I'm a lion!

Don't eat on the run.

Cowboys used to drive large herds of cattle hundreds of miles across the range.

DRAW A COWBOY. Then help him find a lost calf.

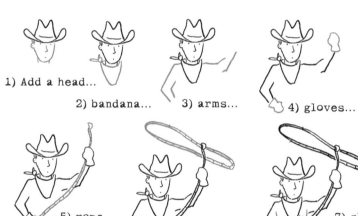

1) Add a head...

2) bandana...

3) arms...

4) gloves...

5) rope...

6) more rope...

7) shirt...

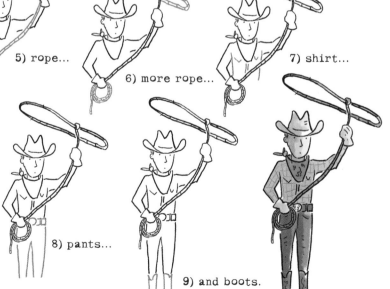

8) pants...

9) and boots.

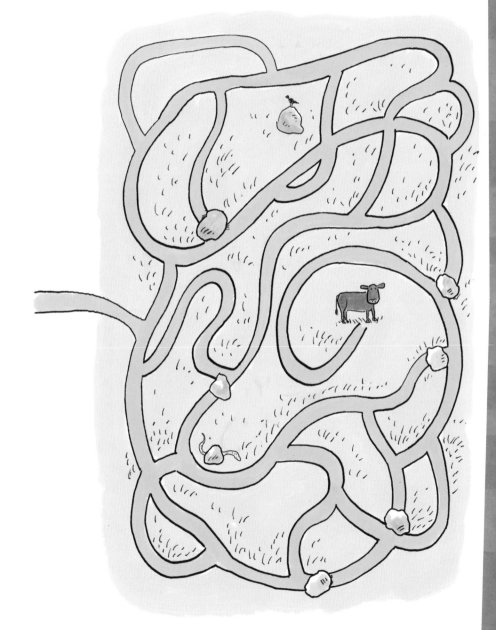

DON'T FLOP AROUND IN YOUR CHAIR.

Fish may flop in a chair, but in the water they're great swimmers.
This picture of Fishy from above shows how she swims by moving her tail.

DRAW FISHY'S TAIL.

Which direction should it go?

DRAW FISHY SWIMMING.

Make Fishy swim back across the page by drawing her four times starting here.

3) a slice on top and two eyes.

2) Add two slices on the sides...

1) Draw a leaf with two curves.

4) Draw the tail curving to one side or another.

DRAW other kinds of fish swimming with Fishy.

USE TWO PAWS

A bear's paw is about the same size as a man's hand, but a bear can't hold its glass the way a human can, because its thumb doesn't bend around opposite to its other fingers.

1) Draw a loop.
2) Add three loops...
3) a thumb loop...
4) two big curves...
5) curves and a shirt.

1) Draw a slice.
2) Add four slices...
3) two squiggly curves...
4) three rows of curves.
5) Add fur.

1) Draw five ellipses...
2) five slices...
3) two squiggly curves...
4) a big blob and ellipse.
5) Add fur.

DRAW A HAND.

Look at the back of your left hand.

Look at the palm of your left hand.

DRAW A PAW.

Look at the back of a bear paw (just kidding!).

DON'T GOBBLE YOUR FOOD.

Who wants to be like a turkey? We're all like turkeys in one way—we're symmetrical, which means that we're the same on one side as on the other.

DRAW HALF A GOBBLER.

Follow the steps below to make this gobbler whole.

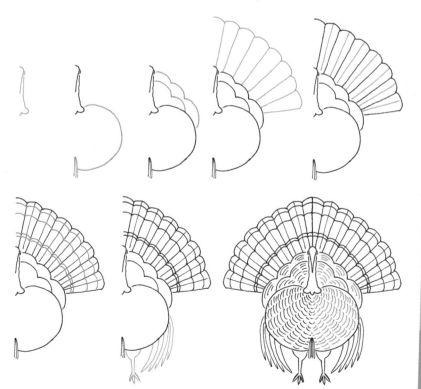

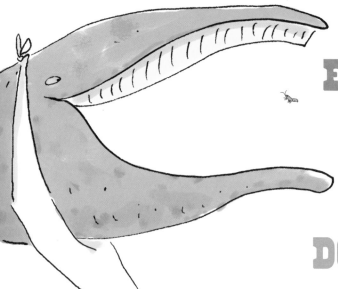

DON'T EAT WITH YOUR MOUTH OPEN.

DON'T SPIT.

The biggest animal on earth, the blue whale, may have the worst manners. First it swims along with its mouth WIDE OPEN, taking in tons of water and tiny creatures called krill. Then it SPITS out the water and swallows the krill—up to 40 million krill every day.

DRAW A KRILL.

1) Draw an O this small.

2) Add a squared U...

3) another squared U...

4) and another...

5) and five more.

6) Draw five pairs of V's...

7) eleven loopy W's...

This is the size of a krill. Now draw 39,999,999 more. That's how much a blue whale eats in one day!

8) a squiggle and nine wavy curves.

Blue whales grow up to 100 feet long, with eyes about this size.

PLEASE PASS THE DOODLES.

Help the octopus pass plates to eight hungry critters. Draw what you think each animal might want to eat on its plate.

DRAW A CATELAFFLY.

Part cat, part elephant, part giraffe, the catelaffly is totally doodle. Follow the steps, or make up your own doodle creature, using parts of different animals.

1) Draw cat ears and eyes.
2) Add an elephant trunk.
3) Attach a giraffe neck.
4) Make butterfly wings.
5) Draw mouse whiskers.
6) Add a dog body...
7) and a bird tail.
8) Walk away on six ant legs.

Please pass the doodle! You can do this doodle on your own or pass it along and take turns drawing each step with others at the table.